NO, NO, NO, NO, NO, YES.
GIDEON AMICHAY

INSIGHTS FROM A CREATIVE JOURNEY

Copyright © 2013 Gideon Amichay, all rights reserved. No part of this book may be reproduced in any manner whatsoever without the written permission of the author except in the case of brief quotations embodied in critical articles and reviews.

Portions of this book are English translations of portions of an original Hebrew version published in Israel in 2011 by Gordon Books, © 2011 Gideon Amichay.

NO, NO, NO, NO, NO, YES is a trademark of No, No, No, No, No, Yes, LLC.

Introduction © 2013 Keith Reinhard
Foreword © 2013 Richard Wilde

Book Design: Raanan Gabriel NYC

Printed in the United States.

ISBN 978-0-9910586-2-4

In memory of my parents, Shlomo and Rachel Amichay.

*Over the years,
whenever someone asked me what my parents do, I'd say:
"Dad sells kindergarten equipment.
Mom is a housewife."*

*These past few years, I realized how wrong I was.
Dad was an entrepreneur, inventing and assembling
thousands of toys with his own two hands.
Mom was my first creative director.*

This book is dedicated to them.

INTRODUCTION

Gideon Amichay defies easy characterization. In appearance he is elegant and soft-spoken. His gentle manner gives no clue to the imagination that rages inside. His mind is a seemingly continuous eruption of original observations and surprising ideas - often brilliant and always provocative.

Though Gideon is a native of Israel now residing in New York, he travels the world, and when asked where he lives, he answers: "I live on Earth." He is a storyteller, an artist, an entrepreneur and a teacher. But most of all, Gideon Amichay is a keen observer who sees the world differently, then arrives at insightful conclusions for us to consider, or imaginative solutions to vexing problems.

I first met Gideon when he was delivering a lecture to a group of graduate students gathered in Cannes, France, as a part of the International Festival of Creativity. The theme of his lecture was the title of this book—*No, No, No, No, No, Yes!* As a firm believer in the omnipotence of persistence, I was taken by Gideon's story of first dreaming of seeing one of his cartoons in The New Yorker, then persisting in realizing that dream in the face of rejection after rejection, until all the "nos" finally evolved into a "yes."

I admire Gideon's ability with both pencil and camera and

his obvious belief that a touch of whimsy not only engages our attention but also helps us understand and remember. And as someone who has spent a lifetime trying to bring creative ideas to life in advertising, I can personally (and painfully!) identify with Gideon's assertion that the cost of creativity, as he puts it, is that we are never truly satisfied.

I like Gideon Amichay because he always makes me think. Readers of this book will be made to think as well. My suggestion is that the book be kept handy as a touchstone for creative people who need a quick and ready dose of inspiration. Open any page of *No, No, No, No, No, Yes!* It will open your mind.

Keith Reinhard
Chairman Emeritus
DDB Worldwide

FOREWORD

No, No, No, No, No, Yes is an amazing story that chronicles Gideon Amichay's rise as a force in the rarefied domain of critical thinking.

In the world of visual communications, Gideon is one of the few individuals who has mastered the art of problem solving, an unteachable discipline. His accomplishments have expanded to include author, entrepreneurialist and teacher.

I've pondered for some time trying to understand how Gideon was able to achieve such success, and the one possible explanation I've come up with to unravel this enigma is a combination of various factors that have resulted in this achievement. By undertaking the seemingly impossible task of creating hundreds and hundreds of conceptual illustrations with the intent of being accepted into, arguably the most difficult venue, *The NEW YORKER* magazine, fostered the emergence of persistence, perseverance and endurance. These qualities were coupled with an essential inner sense of confidence, which can be traced back to what Gideon refers to as his first creative director, his mother, Rachel.

By focusing on illustration and by developing a voice based on conceptual ingenuity, this unique conceptual ability aided Gideon when he undertook the task of being an art director in the world of advertising. He entered this field without any of the dogma that is inherent in advertising education. This gave him the opportunity to embark on projects in the world of advertising with a new and untainted vision. His innovative ideas were challenged again and again, which met with every conceivable "NO", which he took as an opportunity, a challenge that enlivened him and gave meaning to his life. He understood that one must embrace the roadblocks, not react to them, and it is at this very place where his genius emerged and flourished.

Gideon mastered the art of storytelling, which is the foundation of all successful social media. This has become a tool in his arsenal where today, his concepts are so provocative that the media extends his work tenfold.

Gideon has now undertaken the task of educator at both the undergraduate and graduate levels. The courses that he teaches set the stage for others to enter the world of risk taking, love of process, coupled with a spirit to embrace new challenges.

Gideon Amichay understands the pathway toward creativity where he does not have to knock down walls, which is time consuming and unproductive; he knows the secret of how to simply walk around them.

Teaching the intricacies of his journey to others will be Gideon Amichay's legacy.

Richard Wilde
Chair of the Advertising Department at School of Visual Arts New York
Chair of the Design Department at School of Visual Arts New York

NO, NO, NO, NO, NO, YES.

I clearly remember my first NO. As a child I loved sports and became a sprinter and long jumper. I wouldn't say the news sent Carl Lewis into a frenzy, but for my neighborhood in Holon, a small suburban city near Tel Aviv, I guess in a way I was Carl Lewis. I was the school champion. What I wanted most of all, what I desired and lusted after above all else was a pair of Adidas ROMs. Nike didn't exist yet, and the coolest sneakers were the white Adidas with the three blue stripes.

After months of begging, nagging and pleading my father – who'd grown up in a working class neighborhood in downtown Tel Aviv – finally gave in and decided to indulge me. We took a bus from Holon to a sportswear store on Aliya Street in Tel Aviv - the Tel Aviv equivalent of Canal Street. There was no doubt in my mind that my father knew the best store with the best prices.

Yes, if you are wondering, he bought me a new pair of sneakers – simple, grey, no-brand sneakers. They were really nothing to write home about.

Adidas were extremely expensive at the time and looking back on it now, I realize my father made the right decision. Fashion was beyond our means. My father worked hard all his life. My parents invested every penny they earned in education for their children. The most important thing for them was values. Values were far more important than any pair of sneakers. Don't get me wrong, our home lacked nothing, but my parents didn't spend money on luxuries.

Adidas ROMs were a luxury of course, but for me as a child, the whole episode was a tragedy, a crisis, but also a transforming event and a turning point in my life.

At that very moment, my drive came to life. That is where it originated and grew to become my mountain of ambition. It created my endless will to move up and to work hard, usually harder than those around me.

The sneakers I longed for were absolutely everything to me at the time. The rich kids in Tel Aviv came to track competitions wearing Adidas ROMs. I wanted to compete on equal terms. This experience was strengthening, toughening, empowering. It has driven and motivated me ever since.

My ambition is hard to explain because it changes, shifts shape and morphs, continuously adopting different characteristics and objectives.

But it's always there.

My mother was a Jewish mother.

Naturally, my Jewish mother, like all Jewish mothers, wanted me to be a doctor, or a lawyer… or as she used to say, "Be something!"

I wanted to be a cartoonist.
Oy vey, a cartoonist was not on her list...

I was six or seven, and my mother was the critic of my drawings: "I'm not sure about the colors… The composition is well, so-so…"

You can imagine the picture.

At the same time, all the drawing my friends made were instantly put up on their refrigerator doors. Yes, the fridge, the Museum of Kids.

Fast forward to 1989. I am living in New York City.

Paul Peter Porges was my teacher at the School of Visual Arts in New York and a published cartoonist for Mad Magazine and The New Yorker.

The dream of every cartoonist in the world is to have their cartoons published in The New Yorker. That was my dream too.

"There are so many magazines and newspapers. Why do you insist on The New Yorker?" Paul asked me. "It's impossible to get in…Only the top cartoonists make it."

"No chance!"

"But if you insist, you should know that on every Wednesday you can leave an envelope with sketches at The New Yorker reception desk, and you can have it back on Friday."

I didn't need more than that. I drew all day and all night. On Wednesday morning, I walked all the way to The New Yorker and went up to the 22nd floor.

The receptionist gave me "the look", the "I've seen thousands like you" kind of look. Funny, I gave him exactly the same look,"…and I've seen thousands like you". Then he stuck my envelope into a HUGE box full of envelopes.

On Thursday I hardly slept.

On Friday, full of excitement, I rushed to The New Yorker office.

My envelope was waiting for me.
All the sketches were in it, and in the same order.

There was a yellow note from The New Yorker attached to it with a **NO**.

It was an American style apology, explaining that my sketches didn't fit…

On Monday, I showed the note to Paul.
"I told you so." Paul told me so.

(212) 840-3800

> We regret that we are unable to use the enclosed material. Thank you for giving us the opportunity to consider it.
>
> THE EDITORS

The New Yorker was my dream...I went all over the city with my sketch book, drawing more and more sketches. On the next Wednesday, 1 envelope, 20 sketches and 1 me, went to The New Yorker office.

Here is a sketch from that envelope.

FOOD

On Friday another **NO**-yellow-note was waiting for me. Wednesday & Friday, Wednesday & Friday, Wednesday & Friday…

Unwittingly, I had managed to develop a relationship with the receptionist, as in the famous novel by Isaac Bashevis Singer, "Enemies, A Love Story."

I loved the receptionist.
He hated me.

Then, one Friday, there was a surprise. It was the same **NO** yellow note, but there was a scribble on it.

I couldn't read it. It was illegible. (Can you read it?)

That was the moment it hit me. My mother was right! If I had been a doctor, I could have read it!

I asked the receptionist, but he couldn't read it either.

On Monday, Paul was so happy. "That scribble means someone is telling you you're on the right track." The note reads **"Sorry."**

A scribble? It was a masterpiece!

(212) 840-3800

> We regret that we are unable to use the enclosed material. Thank you for giving us the opportunity to consider it.
>
> THE EDITORS

Wednesdays…

Fridays…

Sketches…

And scribbles…

"Keep trying"

You see I could read it now.

THE NEW YORKER
25 WEST 43RD STREET
NEW YORK, N.Y. 10036

(212) 840-3800

> We regret that we are unable to use the enclosed material. Thank you for giving us the opportunity to consider it.
>
> THE EDITORS

If you knew my mother, my real cartoon editor, you would know that there is no cartoon editor in the world that could break me.

No way. I kept trying.

Another week went by, another twenty sketches.

Then, one Friday, one drawing was missing.
The pencil scribble said:

"Holding 1"

What did that mean? Paul knew the answer. "The cartoon editor is keeping 1 sketch for the editorial meeting."

Keeping or not keeping, my excitement kept on for exactly one week.

THE NEW YORKER
25 WEST 43RD STREET
NEW YORK, N. Y. 10036

(212) 840-3800

> We regret that we are unable to use the enclosed material. Thank you for giving us the opportunity to consider it.
>
> THE EDITORS

On the next Friday, I received my envelope with 21 drawings…
20 +1…

Wednesdays & Fridays, Fridays & Wednesdays… sketches & notes, notes & sketches…

"Holding 2"…

During this time, I was still a student at the Bezalel School of Art. After 1 year and 1,000 sketches done when I was living in New York, I had to go back to Israel to present my graduation project. I chose the ten best sketches for my graduation project.

Next, I started on my long career in advertising.

THE NEW YORKER
25 WEST 43RD STREET
NEW YORK, N.Y. 10036

(212) 840-3800

> We regret that we are unable to use the enclosed material. Thank you for giving us the opportunity to consider it.
>
> THE EDITORS

Fast forward to 1993.

Commercial TV had just been introduced in Israel and I was sent by my agency to New York for two weeks. Getting ready to pack, I opened the closet where I kept my winter clothes. I was searching for my scarf and gloves and there it was… the envelope with the sketches from my graduation project.

My dream was alive again.

"I've got nothing to lose!" I told myself. I put the envelope into my suitcase and flew to New York.

Monday, Tuesday, and then on Wednesday at noon, you already know the ritual. I walked all the way to The New Yorker, straight to the top floor. There was a new receptionist, but he gave me the same old look.

On Thursday I got a voicemail. It was the sweetest voice I had ever heard:

"Hi Gideon, this is Ann from The New Yorker.
Could you drop by our office tomorrow?
We would like to discuss some of your drawings."

"Woooooooooooow!!!"

The next day, I saw the receptionist again.
For the first time ever, I walked through the castle gates.

I met Francoise Mouly, in her office at The New Yorker.
All my sketches were leaning against the wall and she said, "We would like to buy that one."

This is my first color drawing published in The New Yorker in 1995.

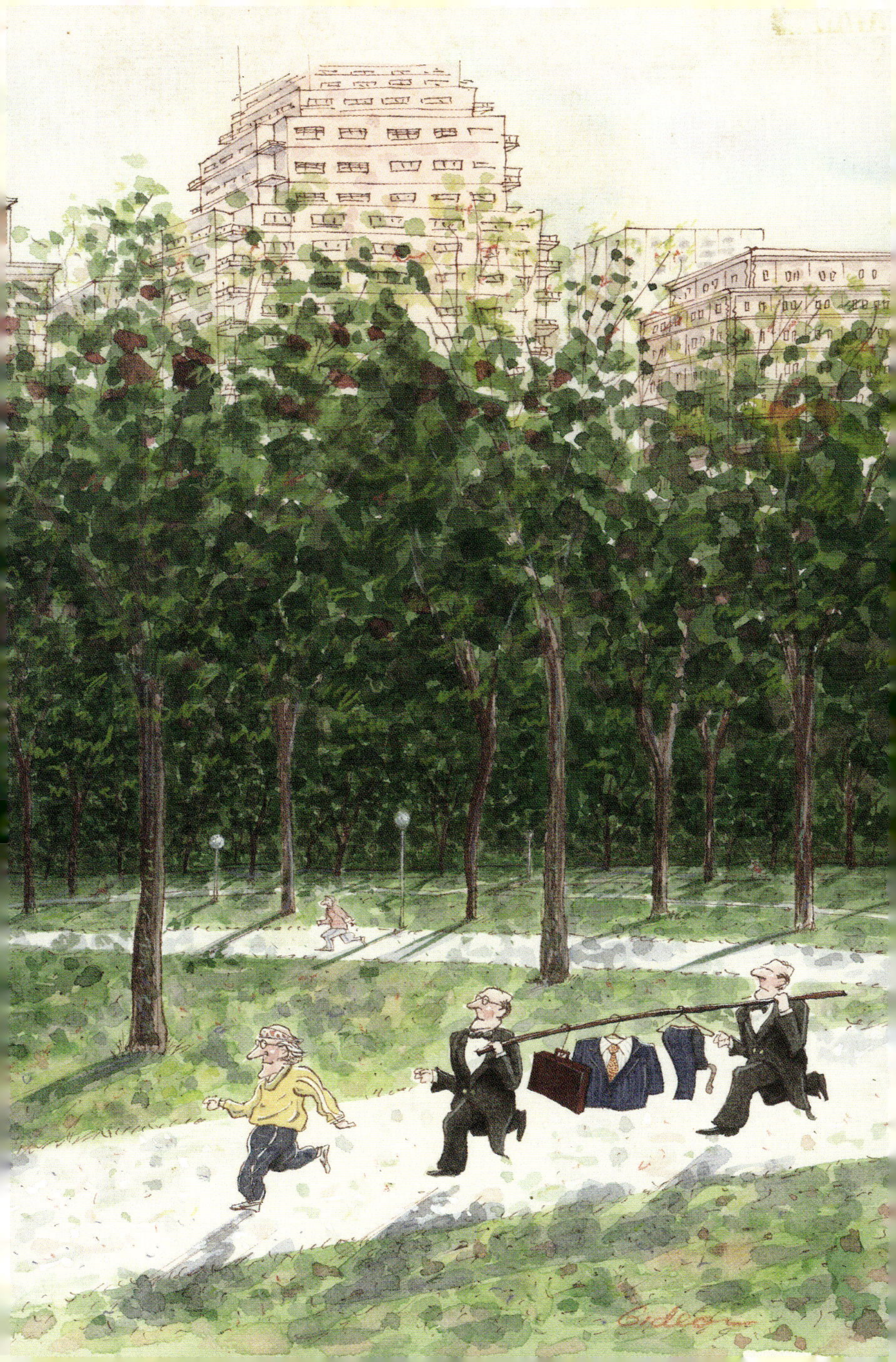

"…and we would also like to buy that one..."
Here is my second drawing, also published in 1995.

Gideau

I left The New Yorker offices and immediately called my mother in Israel:

"Mom, I've got a surprise for you!"
"Is she Jewish?
Are you getting married?
What's her name?" was her answer…

But this is not a story about drawings.

It is a story about one word, full of inspiration:

No!

It's not fun to get a **NO**, really not a pleasure.

CEOs, entrepreneurs, and creative people get all kinds of NOs.

In the beginning I thought every NO was the end of the world, a NO with a big exclamation point!

I might have given up my dream. A big mistake.

The reality is different because NO is a part of life. Usually, **NO** comes with a comma.

No,

Remember, my first NO was just a standard NO.

Then I got a very personal NO comma, "sorry"
NO comma, "keep trying"
NO comma, "holding one"
NO comma, "holding two"

NO, comma.

As in life-
NO comma, "we don't have the time."
NO comma, "we don't have the budget."
NO comma, "can we see another option?"

NO comma, NO comma, NO comma.

We have to examine, to explore, to discover which NO comma we are dealing with.

There are many types of NO commas.
The first is the dramatic NO comma which drives us to work even harder. Then we have the inspirational NO comma which makes us rethink. Finally there's the most challenging NO comma which leads us to change and go in a different direction.

NO comma has great power.
Every NO comma is a treasure.
Every NO comma is a great opportunity to search for the next YES.

No no No No no No No No No No No No No No No No No no No No no Yes no no

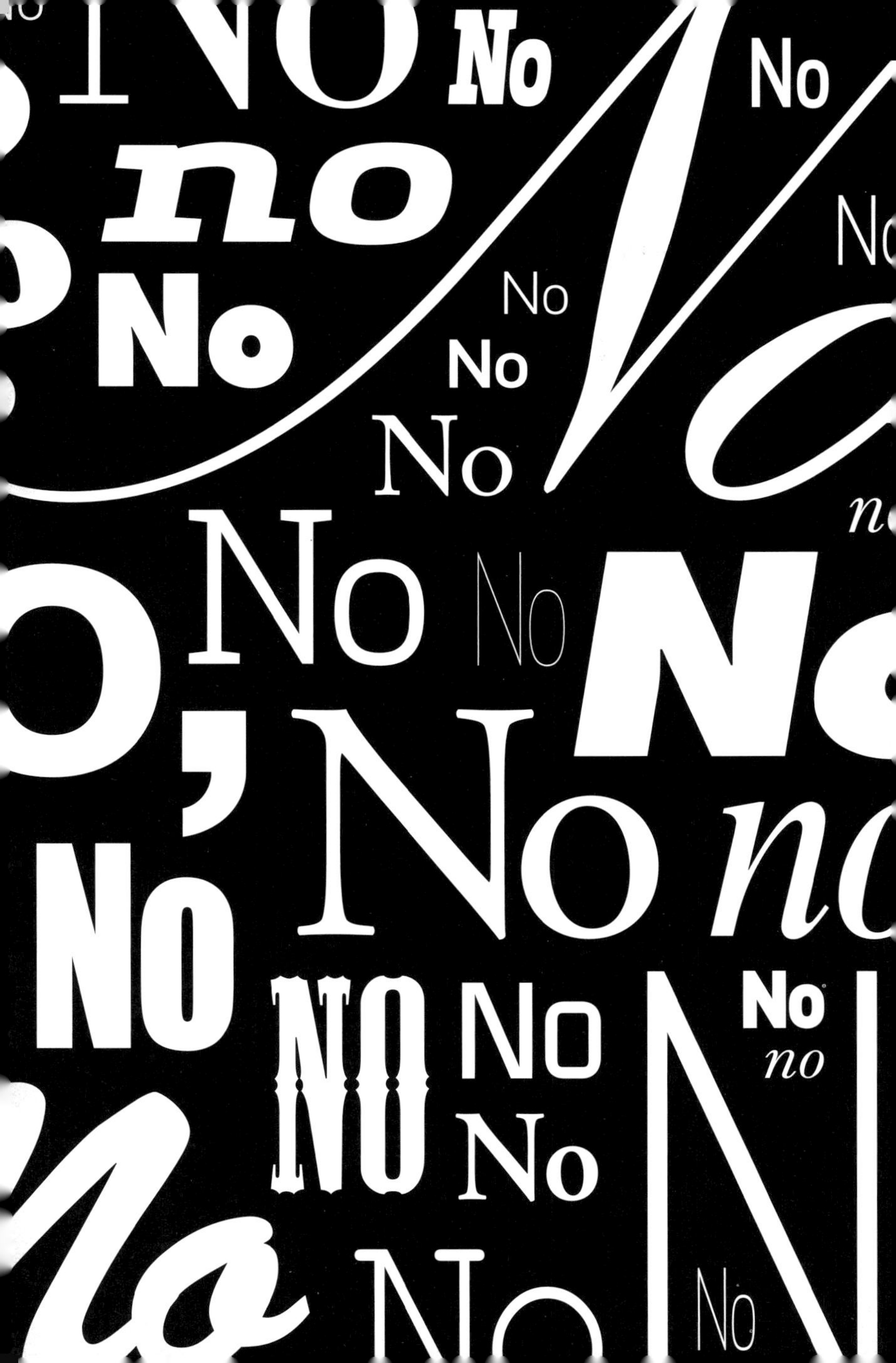
No
No
No
no
No
No
No
No
No
No
No
No
no
No
No
No
No
No
no
No
No

By the way, there is one YES on the previous page.

Did you spot it?

No?

Actually almost every **NO** comes with a question mark.

NO?

Really?
Really!

I've developed a relationship with NO.
I hug it, I embrace it and I nurture it. I care for it. I've even grown to love it.

Resistance is good. Resistance in innovation, in hi-tech, in art, etc. is great.

For me, NO is a sign, a green light and not a red light.
NO is the beginning of a YES.

My life in advertising at Shalmor Avnon Amichay Y&R in Israel introduced me to many more types of NO commas.

The following is dedicated to destroyers of ideas, wherever they may be. They are the ones who say NO, time after time, instead of trying to spot and discover the invisible comma.

I am addressing all of the
"No comma, I'm afraid that..." men
and all of the
"No comma, I'm worried that…" women.

I am speaking to all the
"No comma, it won't work" people
and to all the providers of excuses wherever they are and whoever they may be.

To all fearers of fear of the unknown…
It's easy to be a skeptic.
It's easy to play it safe.
It's easy to remain undecided.

Which of these three is the worst? It's hard to determine.

Obviously, it's easier not to do anything. It won't bother anyone and no one will complain. In most cases, doing nothing won't make a mess. Logic dictates that we should keep on doing what was done by others before us and then things will continue as before. If there is a problem we will always be able to blame the decision makers of the past.

My first NO commas came from the people around me. I was surrounded by creative people and so it came as a big surprise to me to see their skepticism alive and kicking. I thought it was more usual to see that kind of behavior from business people, but I was wrong.

Finding excuses is part of life everywhere...
It's a cultural issue.

During the years I worked in advertising, I led a project for Dannon yogurt in Israel. As part of a new marketing campaign, Dannon wanted to get closer to consumers. The idea was to make real people become part of the brand's image – real people not models. It was decided to put the photo of a real consumer on every Dannon package. We invited people to upload their picture on a Dannon cup to a special web site where votes would be cast. The highest rated consumers' photos would be featured on Dannon cups at the supermarkets. People loved it. More than 100,000 different people uploaded their pictures. It was crazy. Votes came in from 157 different countries. Everyone was happy.

Well, almost everyone.

Big NO commas had come from the creative people around me. They were not sure that enough people would participate. The most surprising NO comma had come from the campaign photographer. "I'm afraid we won't have enough good looking people… we won't have diversity… real consumers can't act in front of the camera… etc. etc. etc."

It was clear my first mission would be to change the creative culture. There was a need to create the right environment for how to treat a NO among the creative people around me and then with all of our creative collaborators as well.

We discovered that whenever we could define the comma, we achieved better results in the end.

The next challenge was dealing with NO's from the client's side. Clients say NO many times, that's part of life. Exploring the comma had a huge effect on everyone. It built a culture of exmination and, in time, I discovered it was a great way to find the path to a YES.

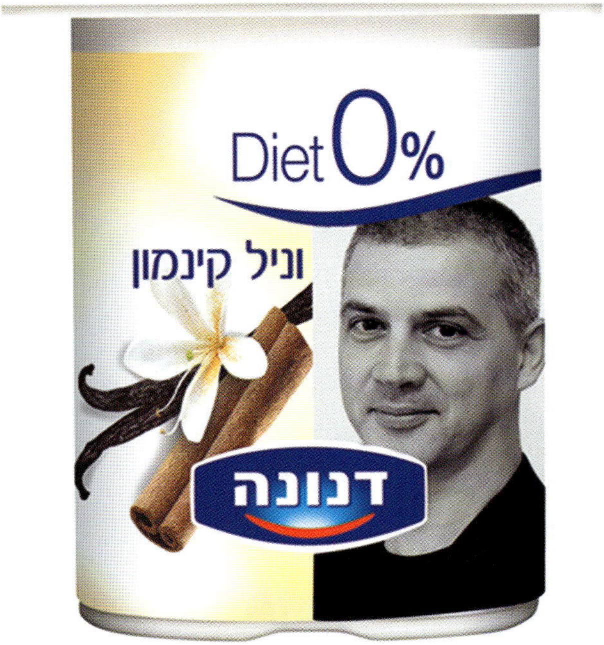
Diet 0%
וניל קינמון
דנונה

In 2007, the agency had an advertising idea for Orange mobile company. The management of Orange loved it, but at the same time they had a huge problem with the idea's message. I don't believe in problems, so let's say they were greatly challenged by it. Orange was the first mobile brand to deal with the danger of texting while driving. Now it's a clear and unquestionable message, but back then, it was a pioneering idea.

The discussion had many types of NO's:
"NO, texting-and-driving is a problem, but…"
"NO, it's a no-go zone…"
"NO, it's not our job (the mobile company's job) to bring up that issue…"
"NO, texting is great business for us." etc…

It was a NO, but there was also a comma.

I could see the comma in the behavior of the Orange people. The importance of the message was clear. While their mouths said NO, their body language betrayed them. I could see them moving uncomfortably in their chairs. It was a pioneering message and they knew it.

In the end, understanding that comma led us to propose only a print ad. It was a solution everyone could live with. We didn't propose a billboard campaign or a TV spot, just a print ad. Orange had the guts to be a pioneer for an uneasy message, but only on a limited scale.

Seven months later, that print ad won Israel's first ever Cannes Lion print award. Needless to say, Orange continued to support this message in the coming years.

text
messaging
while
driving
prevents
you from
seeing what
really
matters.

orange

Those of you who may have worked with media people, probably agree with me that there is a notion that the media doesn't say no to money. That is not true. They don't say no to easy money. I learned that lesson from a Yellow Pages billboard campaign.

For many years, a billboard campaign was easy money for media companies. Sell a package of a thousand billboards, project the image in all different sizes and that's it, a home run, nothing to it.

What if every billboard was uniquely produced?

TIRE REPAIR

חפש

פנצ'ר

co.il
מספר 1 בחיפה

M
מרקעים

Now, that's not easy money.

In the media companies, NO's shot up like mushrooms after a rain.

But these were just NO commas. Fortunately, the campaign idea was well defined and engaging, and it offered a relevant solution for Yellow Pages. The key to getting a YES was simple. We offered the billboard companies acknowledgment and credit along with us for pioneering innovative outdoor media solutions and developing unique billboards.

MAGNETS

78 PRIVATE INVESTIGATORS

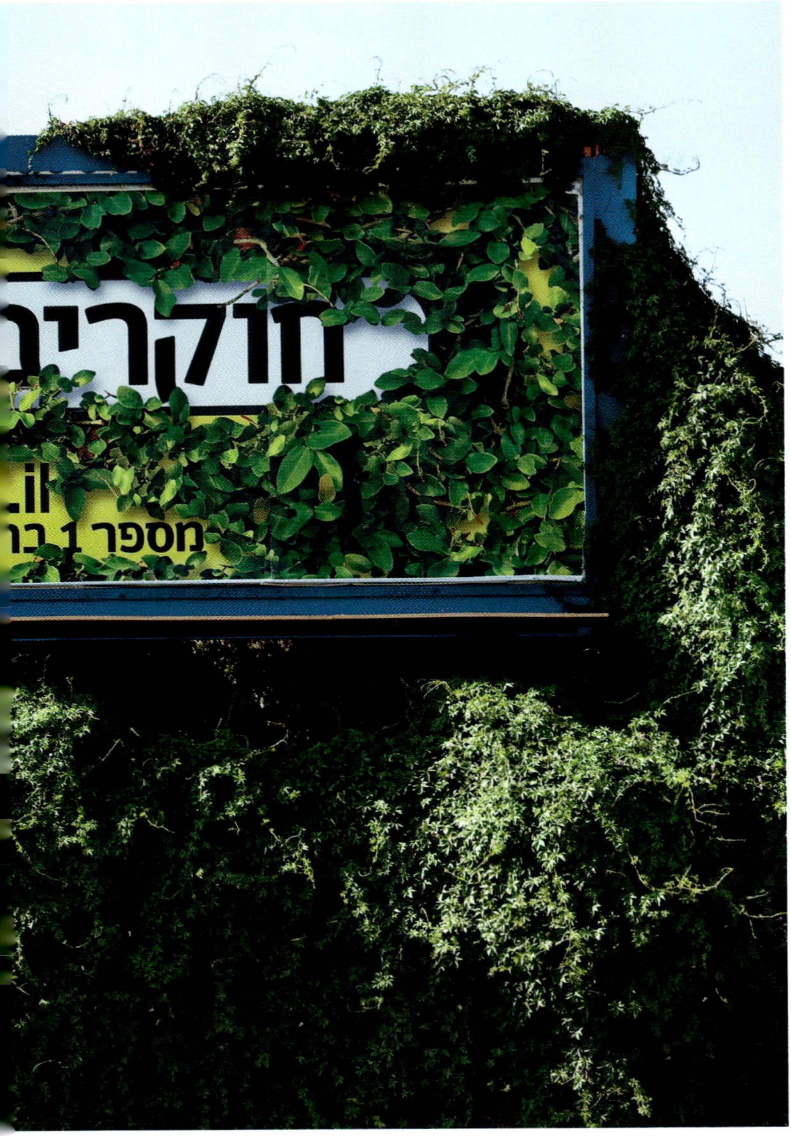
מספר 1

One night, the phone in my office rang.
On the other end of the line was Moshe Nur, the owner of Nur Star Media.

"Hi Gideon…"

Moshe and I had known each other for twenty years, but this time his tone was different.

"Yes, Moshe," I replied, puzzled.

Nur's billboards have a unique format. They are different from the others. His billboards are vertical, whereas all the others on the market are horizontal, like a TV screen.

Moshe said, "Your friends in the ad industry keep telling me there is no way to create vertical billboard copy. I want to change that mind set forever. I'm open to ideas, any ideas."

"Who's the client?" I asked.

"My company, Nur Star media" he said. "Let's put your ideas to good use. Let's do a pro-bono campaign against drunk driving."

At the next agency innovation meeting I laid out the assignment:
"Please bring ideas you think we cannot do."

A week later, we had more than fifty ideas. Most of them were interesting and some were really good. There was one team, Ran Cory and Paul Paszkowski, who came up with an idea that really met the challenge – an icon of a bottle made up of crashed cars. Simulated in Photoshop, it was a strong icon and it fit the vertical billboard shape.

I thought it was a brilliant idea, but I felt we could take it one step further.

"Why don't we make it real?" I asked.

"What do you mean real?" they replied. "There is NO way…"

Oh boy, do I love these moments.

"Sure there is. Let's make it real, a real life installation," I shot back. They smiled. I'm not sure I was that sure myself, but at least I tried to act as if I was.

A week later we met with Moshe Nur and presented him with our three final ideas. The bottle was the fourth one. Since I considered it to be so different, I didn't think it was right to present it along with the others.

I had doubts whether Moshe would like it. I also had a tiny doubt about its feasibility, which is why I didn't really push hard for it. The idea had to sell itself, which it did. Moshe didn't panic when he saw the presentation. At least he didn't seem to show it.

He didn't say NO.
And he didn't say YES either.
But we all felt the comma.

We didn't know how to pull it off. Literally, we didn't have a clue. We were in the "we don't know zone," a new type of comma, a new kind of headache.

83

Later that week, we discussed the "how" not the "if" of the project. We erased all the NO's and all the commas. We had a goal to strive for. It took us six months. We went through the slow process of building the billboard, buying the crashed cars, soldering them together, and then finding a place for the installation. We had already gotten a NO from the Tel Aviv municipality. When the billboard was almost completed, Nur asked our permission to involve "Or Yarok", the association for Safer Driving in Israel. "Sure, go for it" I said without hesitating.

The original plan was to have the billboard in place for three months, but it stayed there for two years.

אם שותים
לא נוהגים!
אור ירוק
העמותה לשינוי תרבות הנהיגה בישראל
נור

There will always be NO people and NO comma people. There will always be people who will put brakes on your ideas, who will try to demoralize you by looking for easy ways out, and who will wave an annoying "I told you so" banner. These same people then try to ride on the coattails of your project when it succeeds.

If the idea is really great, relevant and uplifting, there is a chance that at a certain moment those NO people will be caught off guard. They will get carried away and will be infected by your faith and optimism.

In a world that is becoming faster and crueler, one should dream more. One should initiate far more special, exceptional and different projects. Ideas that make everyone ask "How did you pull it off? How did you make it happen?"

Please bring ideas you think we cannot do.

NO commas are universal, they exist everywhere. Every time you think you've overcome them a new one emerges – different, challenging, and novel.

Early in 2010, I felt I had reached a critical point in my life and I found myself having to deal with a new and unknown type of NO comma. It was an inner NO comma, a personal one. At that point in my career, I thought I had already made the acquaintance of every type of NO comma up close and on a personal level. But it seems I was wrong.

Until then, NO commas came from all around me, from my family, my colleagues and the clients I worked with. This one was different. It felt different. It was the first time a NO comma had come from my guts. I guess there's a first time for everything.

The agency was doing really well. I had worked day and night for sixteen years and everything was running smoothly, in fact the best it ever had. I felt I needed to move on, to find my next challenge.

"NO way, I can't do that! This is my home! This is my identity! This is who I am."

All year long that was the answer I gave myself while the comma kept growing louder and more insistent.

"NO comma, your name is on the door, you can't resign from your own agency."

The day-to-day pressure and workload didn't help.
I needed to clear my mind and to get a fresh perspective.
I decided to fly to Zurich to meet with my mentor, Michael Conrad. I knew Michael through the Berlin School of Creative Leadership. When you need thought provoking conversation, Michael is your man. He is honest and full of wisdom, a mentor if I ever met one.

For years I had passed through the Zurich airport but I had never actually seen the city. I imagined it to be Swiss, business oriented, bland and boring. After a ten minute train ride I was in the center of the city. Zurich is small, tiny in fact, but charming and filled with exquisite European atmosphere.

Michael's captivating smile met me at the entrance to his house which is up on the mountain that overlooks Zurich. The house was exactly as I'd imagined, warm, radiating optimism, full of paintings, photographs and touching reminders of his great career. Michael had been the global creative director of Leo Burnett, the world renowned advertising agency.

Each painting in his house told a story, sometimes a whole book. It is pointless to try to put into words the sparkle that lit up his eyes when he told a story about a particular painting. Sometimes imagination just works better.

Then Michael said "let's go to my meeting room."

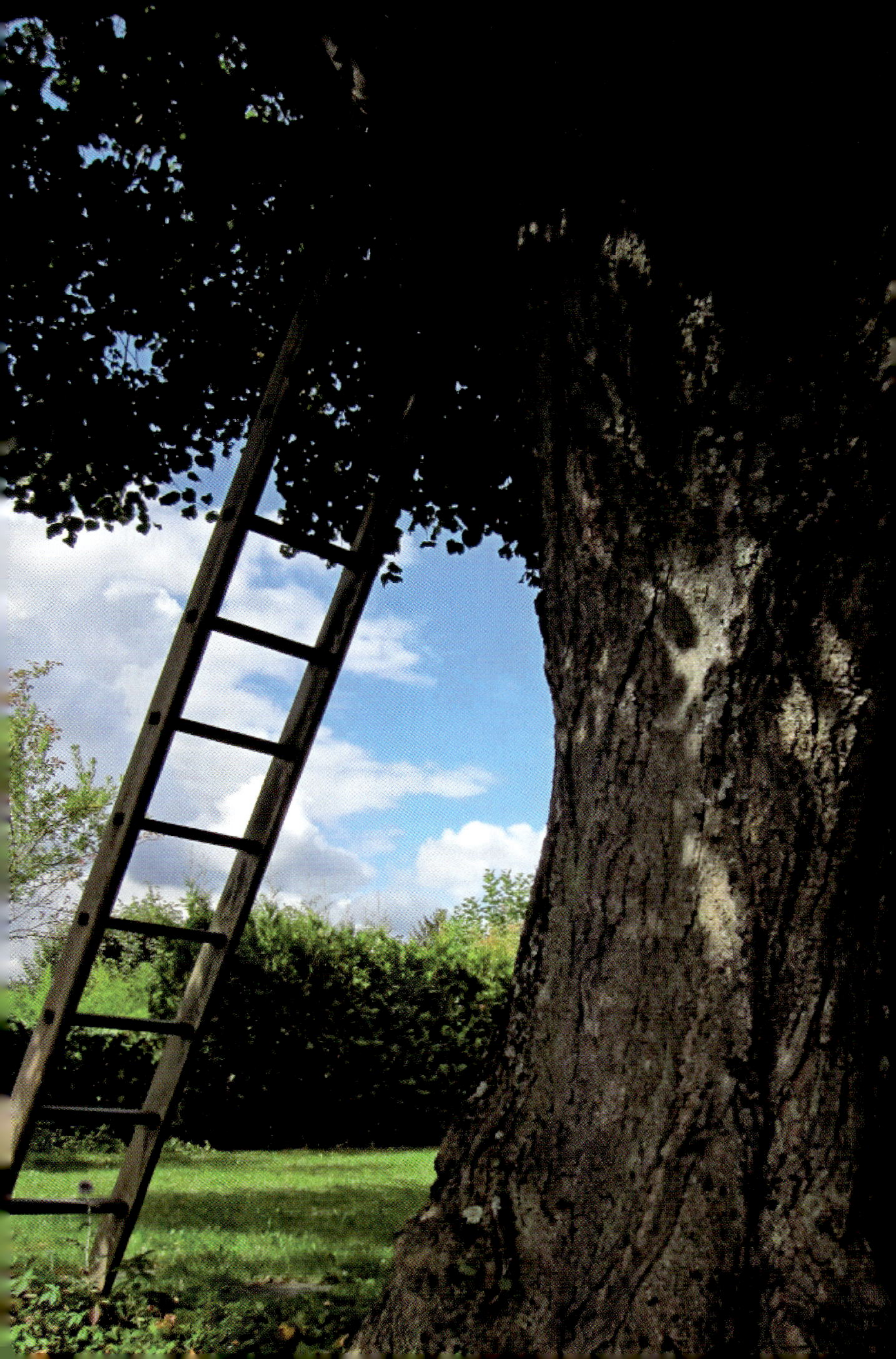

Naturally, I presumed he meant the room next door. Loaded with wine, two glasses and an abundance of goodies, instead we went outside to the yard. "Maybe the meeting room is on the other side of the house," I thought to myself trying to figure out the logic behind walking into the yard. Then I noticed that he had stopped and I took in the view of our meeting room in all of its glory. The ladder that led to it and the vista from it left no doubt that this was the perfect meeting room for our conversation.

"Michael," I said, "it's about my job. I'm about to resign from Shalmor Avnon Amichay/Y&R, and it's hard. Hell, I've been there almost all my life and I'm a partner. It's crazy. My name is on the door. I can't bring myself to do it."

Michael listened carefully, from time to time punctuating my monologue with some thoughtful comment. Then he shared with me some stories from his own life experience. He asked me many questions. I didn't have all answers. Even now, three years later, I'm not sure I've got all of them.

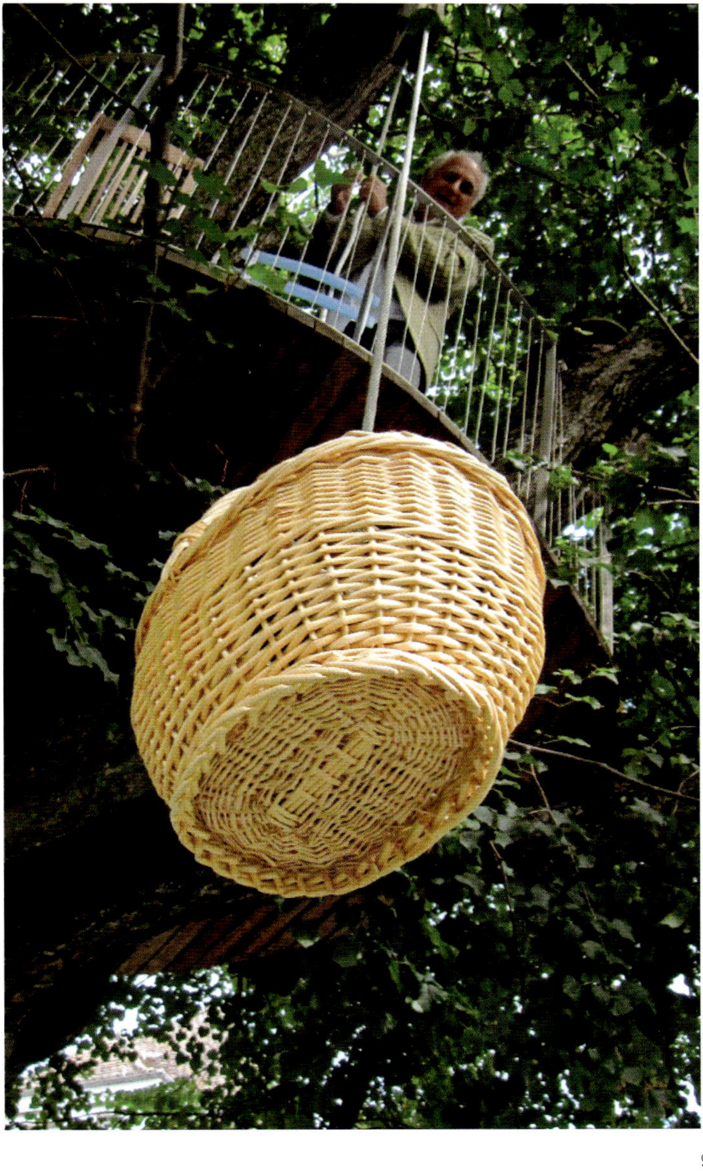

On the red-eye flight back to Israel, I hardly slept. I ran our conversation back in my head over and over again. Only one question stuck in my mind all night long, but it was the right one, "Do you still enjoy being there?"

By the next morning, the NO comma was gone.
I handed in my resignation.

In 2011, after eighteen years with my agency, I started to assemble the material for this book. This gave me the opportunity to come back to drawing, my first love.

As I was going through my submission sketches to The New Yorker from 1989, I came upon this one.

A smile lit up my face.

I felt exactly the way I had when I first drew it.
I'm still climbing the mountain I thought to myself.

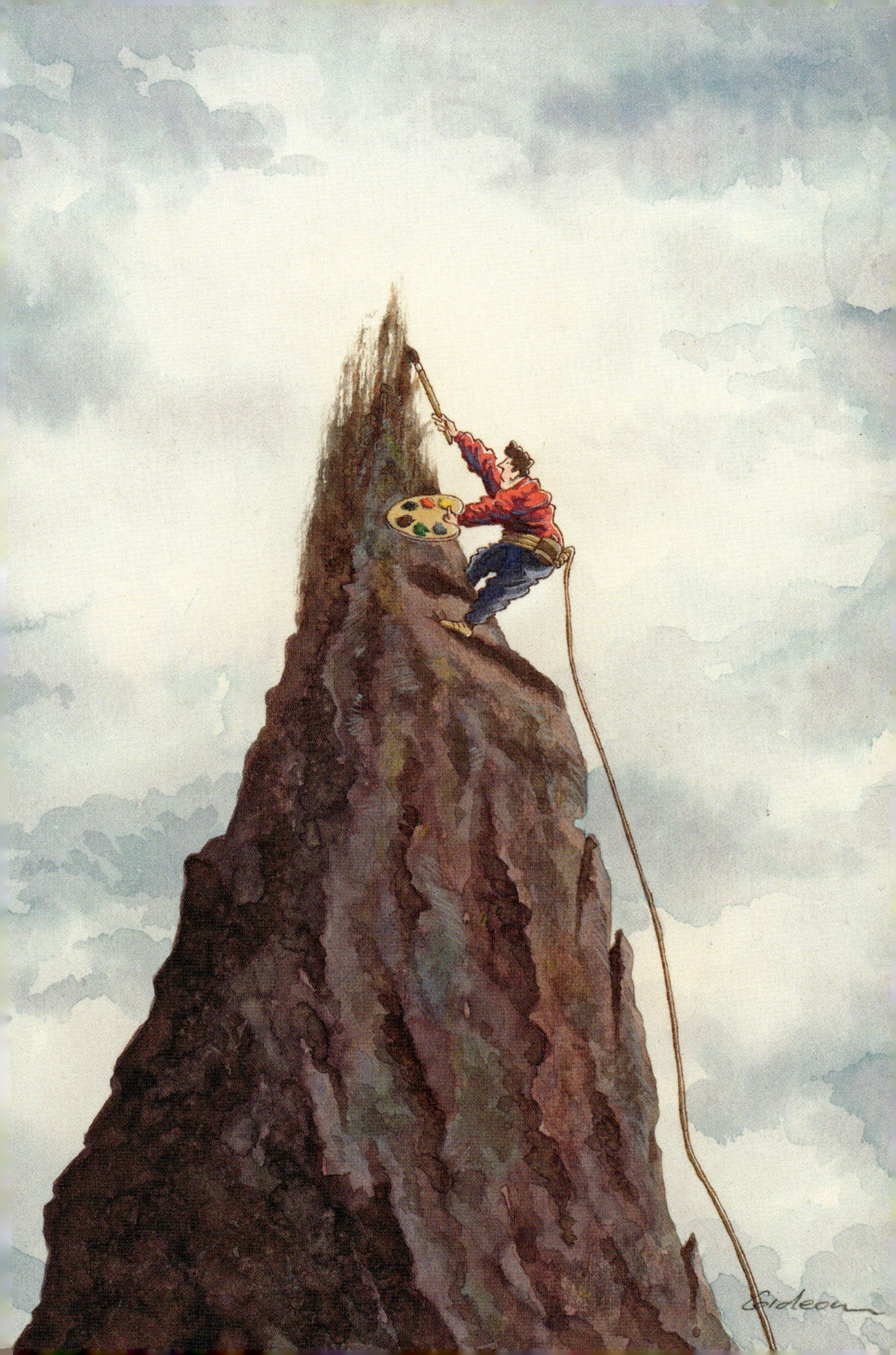
Gideon

And then I saw the last drawing from 1989.

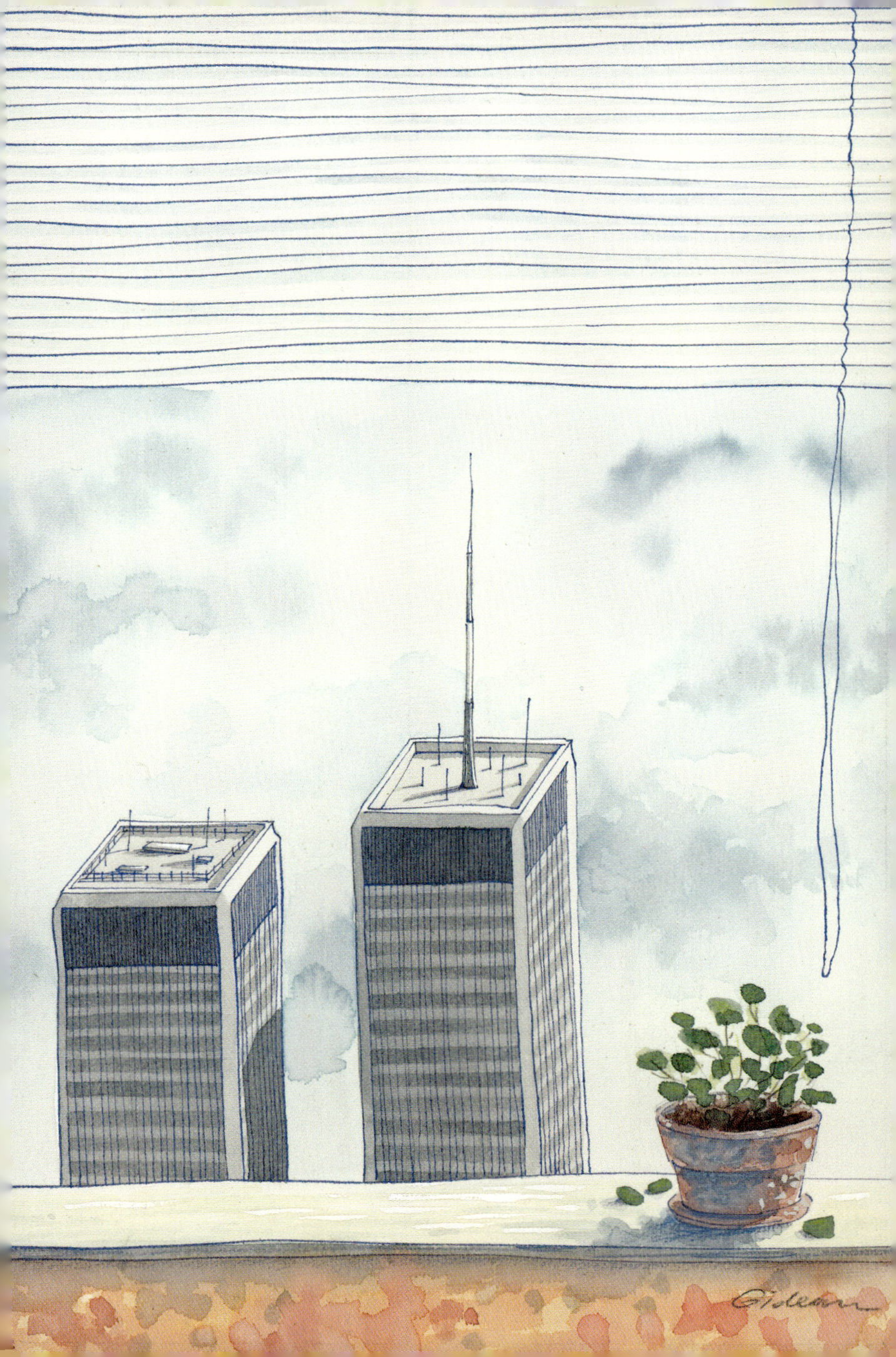

Back then, when I was living in New York City, I remember coming out of the subway and seeing them for the very first time -

THE TWIN TOWERS

They were astonishing. I was moved.

My idea was to draw them from another angle - from above. Let's say 100 floors above. I thought that was an original idea. A naive look at the Twin Towers from a rear window.

On September 11th 2001 that drawing took on a different meaning. It became a scary look from the rear window. The feeling bothered me a lot, but I didn't know what to do with it.

Ten years after 9/11, that drawing still troubled me.

Now I thought it was about time that I did something with it, so I emailed the drawing to The New Yorker.

No answer at all.

I couldn't find peace for my soul.

I decided to change the drawing to a different medium. I created a short video out of it. It became a thirty second animation movie with the title,
"9/11. It's been ten years."

My name and the Israeli flag were on the last frame.

9/11
It's been ten years

01

03

02

04

05

07

06

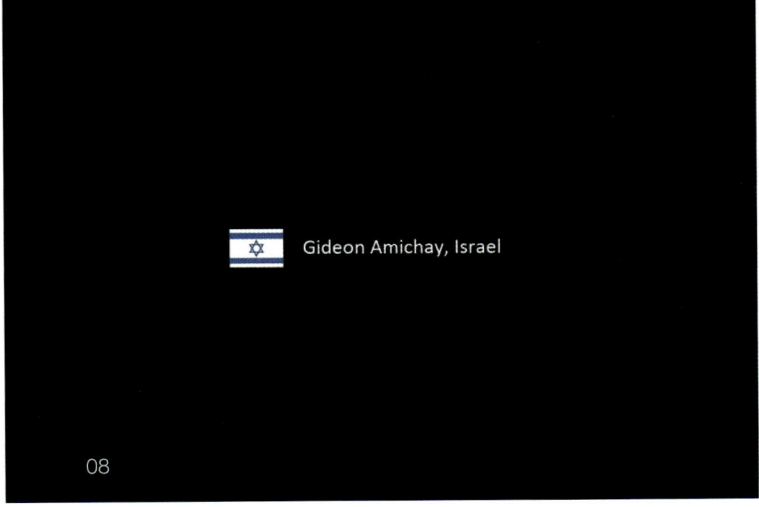

08

Gideon Amichay, Israel

Then I had another idea for a larger project. I called Uri Shinar from ANIBOOM, which is a virtual animation studio. Together, we invited video artists to create short animation clips based on the theme of **"9/11. It's been ten years."**

After three months we had clips from 20 countries.

The next step was to find a real life venue for the project. I'm not going to share with you how many NO's we got from TV channels, galleries and museums. Believe me, we got dozens of NO's.

Finally, in February of 2012, I was invited to deliver a presentation to the curators of the 9/11 Memorial Museum at Ground Zero.

I didn't do a presentation. I told them a story, the story about the drawing that you just read.

March

April

May

June

July

August

Nine months later, on 9/11 2012 – talk about symbolic– the very same day – I got an email from the museum with a proposed 5 year contract to show the animation project as part of the opening of the 9/11 Memorial Museum.

After 23 years, the drawing might have found its final resting place.

No, No, No, No, No… Yes, in the end.

We need to believe, sometimes even to change direction.

We need patience.

We are all students at the faculty of patience. There is always another semester.

But finally, this is not a story about drawings.
It is about a relationship with NO.

So, what is your relationship with NO?

Sadly, my mother died eight years ago.

This drawing, I believe, would have made it to her fridge.

ACKNOWLEDGMENTS

Huge thanks to my elder brothers, the late talented and creative Yossi and Motti, who supported me and my chosen road through all the family disputes - "Learn some profession, will you!"

Thanks to Zeev the late cartoonist who taught me to love cartoons so much. Thanks to Paul Peter Porges who taught me to see the masterpiece in the scribbles. Thanks to Amnon Be-Rav, my first editor who gave my first chance. Thanks to Amram Prat and Shimon Zandhauz who convinced me to study at the Bezalel Academy of Arts and Design. Thanks to Avi Eisenstein who so rightly insisted that I would not remain merely a cartoonist forever. Thanks to Yarom Vardimon who always instills the fear of a professor in me. Thanks to Guy Billout who taught me how to think differently. Thanks to David Tartakover - each moment spent in his presence is real magic. Thanks to Zvi Levin who I wanted to be like when I was young. Thanks to Reuven Adler for the shout from across the street that changed my entire career. Thanks to Shmuel Warshavski who opened a door to the world of advertising for me.

Special thanks to Rami Shalmor and Shlomi Avnon, my partners for over 18 years. Together we all reached new heights. Thanks to the copywriters, art directors, designers, account executives, photographers, producers, directors, editors, musicians with whom I've had the privilege to learn how to make all dreams come true. They are all super talented people.

I thank Zipa Kempinsky, my Israeli book editor. She encouraged me to take up drawing again after a break of 20 years. A special thanks to Amir Hadad a friend and talented publisher. Thanks also to Tirza Ben Porat and Tal Boniel who worked with him.

To Michael Conrad, a man of vision and inspiration, thanks for teaching me how to reinvent myself. A special thanks to Keith Reinhard and Richard Wilde for their constant support. Thanks to Priscilla Karnat, my English teacher, for being so tough with me.

Thanks to my friends for charging me with new energy for this journey - Ido Aharoni, Oded Gera, Shai Sagie, Eran Gefen, Vered Mosenzon, Shai Almagor, Eva Hasson, Ehud Arnon, Edo Segal, Ziv Navoth, Vico Sharabani, Lior Zoref, Daniel Nissan, Maya Yeshurun, Zviah Eldar, Yoram Altman, Linda Langton, Haim Teller, Anja Waleson, Abigail Tenembaum and Michael Weitz.

And finally I send a huge hug, to the enthusiastic and energetic Sivia Loria, my book editor, for challenging me with thoughtful advice.

PICTURE CREDITS

Drawings on pages 15-19, 26, 33, 36, 99, 101, 104-107 by Gideon Amichay.

Drawings on pages 47 and 49 by Gideon Amichay © The New Yorker and The Cartoon Bank 1995.

Photos: Motti Amichay (page 21), Gideon Amichay (pages 44, 93, 95), Menachem Reiss (page 128).

Animation of drawings on pages 104-107 by Ilan Manor.

Dannon "Real People" project on page 69 by Shalmor Avnon Amichay Y&R. **International Awards:** Cannes Lions Shortlist, Gold Effie Award (Israel).

Chief Creative Officer- Gideon Amichay. Executive Creative Director - Yoram Levy. Creative Director - Nadav Persman. The Creative team - Guy Margalit and Lior Zaid. Head of Planning Group - Noam Manela. Planner - Ayelet Asformas. Account executives - Tal Yoffe Fishbein, Sivan Fishler and Liron Ben Yaacov. Graphic design studio - Noga Sifroni. Agency Producers - Shira Robas, Marina Akilov and Racheli Meshulam. Pre-press production - Meyshav Productions. Client – Strauss Dannon Israel.

Orange "Text Messaging" print ad on page 71 by Shalmor Avnon Amichay Y&R. **International awards:** Cannes Bronze Lion, Epica Bronze Medal.

Chief Creative Officer - Gideon Amichay. Executive Creative Director - Tzur Golan. Creative Director - Yariv Twig. Copywriter - Geva Kochba. Art Director - Asaf Covo. Account executives - Merav Harel, Tal Cohen and Merav Greenstein. Client - Orange Israel.

Yellow Pages Billboards campaign on pages 74-79 by Shalmor Avnon Amichay Y&R. **International Awards:** 2 Gold Eurobest, One Show Merit, Cannes Lions Shortlist Gold World Medal - New York Festivals.

Chief Creative Officer - Gideon Amichay. Executive Creative Director -Tzur Golan. Creative Director - Yariv Twig and Amit Gal. Copywriters - Sharon Refael, Paul Paszkowski and Eyal Padan. Art Directors - Gil Aviyam, Ran Cory, Asaf Covo and Shirley Bahar. Account Executives - Adam Avnon, Shiran Chen Barazani, Galia Ashri and Keren Hershkovitz. Head of Planning Group - Hila Tamir. Planner - Zohar Reznik. Photographer - Menachem Reiss. Client - Yellow Pages Israel.

Crashed Cars Bottle project on pages 83-85 by Shalmor Avnon Amichay Y&R. **International Awards:** Communication Arts Annual Award, Cannes Lions shortlist, Golden Drum.

Chief Creative Officer - Gideon Amichay. Executive Creative Director - Tzur Golan - Creative Director - Amit Gal. Art Director - Ran Cory. Copywriter - Paul Paszkowski. Client - Or Yarok / Nur Star Media - Moshe Nur

BIO

Gideon Amichay is an award winning ad man, communication artist, writer and TEDx speaker.

Amichay is known as the person who put Israel on the world advertising map. For 18 years he was a partner at Shalmor Avnon Amichay Y&R. As Chief Creative Officer, Amichay led the agency to become Israel's market leader in creativity and innovation. It was one of the biggest ad agencies in Israel and the most successful Israeli ad agency worldwide. For over 10 years he was also a member of the Worldwide Creative Board of Young & Rubicam. Amichay won hundreds of international awards among them 19 Cannes Lions and 9 Clios for advertising and innovation in communication. He also won a Special Award from the UN.

He started his career as a cartoonist, publishing in the major Israeli newspapers as well as in The New Yorker. His work was displayed in Israel in 2011 at The Holon Design Museum.

Amichay is an international lecturer at universities including the School of Visual Arts in New York, the Hebrew University of Jerusalem, Tel Aviv University and others. In 2012 he served as the President of the Direct Jury at the 2012 Cannes Lions Festival. He graduated from the Bezalel Academy of Arts and Design with honors and earned an MBA from the Berlin School of Creative Leadership.

Gideon Amichay lives and works in NYC.

NO, NO, NO, NO, NO, NO, YES, NO,